The Feather Variations

Poems

Jane Richards

To Elvira,

Jane Richards

Cover design by Travis Morgan
Cover artwork and text illustrations by Melissa Pierson
Author photo by Tim Keane

ISBN: 979-8-9901390-0-8

CARDINAL LANE PRESS
cardinallanepress@gmail.com

TABLE OF CONTENTS

I

Wolf Moon 3

North Country Trail, *O-Kun-de-Kun Falls*............... 4

The Bluebird Trail 5

Sentry 6

In the Season of the Snow Moon 7

Liminal Space 9

Lunar Eclipse, *January 19, 2019* 10

The Mariana Trench 11

II

Ice Storm 15

Lion Sister 16

Ghazal of the Lost Necklace 17

When autumn first opens its hand 18

Why I go to the ocean when life veers into disorder ... 19

The Text on Malicious Magic 20

The Feather Variations 22

TABLE OF CONTENTS

III

Lament of the Dandelion Seed 27

Art in the Time of COVID – 19 28

Tropical Wonderland 29

At Starved Rock 31

Serengeti Pilgrimage 32

Summer Sonatina 33

On the deck one August morning 34

The Dance Unending 35

On Turning 71 36

Cloud Forest 37

I

Wolf Moon

She has been with us three nights—
under clear skies she emerges unblemished,
unrolls her luminous carpet across January snow,
her fingers tracing precise outlines—
tangled branches,
tree trunks in dark columns.

In the woods—
bones exposed,
mute,
our refuge from the bruises of loss—
we wait for the greening,
the hum of trees breathing.

The hour before dawn
the moon arrives at our window,
spreads strong hands across our bed.
Prodding us from old darkness
we awaken inside her canescent embrace,
trace the features on each other's face.

North Country Trail
O-Kun-de-Kun Falls

Familiar friend, this overgrown trail—
we pick its blueberries,
identify its ferns,
whistle to its vireos,
skirt its bear tracks.

Skipping over tree roots,
we sing silly songs in bad French;
and when we hear the falls, shout,
hurry to feel the thunder in our bones,
bask on sandstone flats,
mist cleansing our sweat.

This place, planted in our memories;
the path, imbued with its history:
maple leaf, once scarlet, now a bit of soil,
aster seed, awaiting rebirth,
boot prints, planted with our delight.

The Bluebird Trail

One spring I monitored bluebird boxes.
Every week I would open the panels and peer inside,
scan the darkness, count and record,
while from a nearby branch
an azure-feathered parent watched,
fretting.

The nests, well-crafted as an Amish bed,
cradled blue eggs one week,
hatchlings the next—
the open yellow beaks a bouquet in full bloom,
each attached to a small sack of ashen skin,
lumpy with bones.

Limp bodies grew down the color of first light,
then wild quills poked out all akimbo.
The nestlings took on heft and form.
Now my intrusions prompted them to hunker down,
wing to wing in the cramped quarters,
still as stones.

When the feathers gleamed like dew,
I knew the day of fledging approached;
I was not prepared for the swiftness of their departure.
I shut the abandoned home,
rejoicing—yes!—but not before a moment,
fretting.

Sentry

A big-hearted oak keeps its post
next to the trail,
so old two of me with outstretched arms cannot encircle it,
distorted by branches amputated
for power lines,
withered limbs hanging dark against the sky…

still, still

it sprouts new growth
and on this spring day pushes out
tiny lobed leaves that will darken,
grow large enough to hide birds' nests
while the bark's deep furrows hold safe
secret lives of butterflies and I cannot pass without
stopping,
caressing the craggy trunk wondering
at the cluster of young sprouts,
the relentless insistence.

In the Season of the Snow Moon

I.
I awaken in her gaze
icy as a frozen river,
watch her roll out a harsh tongue of light,
a truth-teller baring aging snow—
flakes that once drifted from the heavens,
twirling lace delicate and pure,
now no more than dirty t-shirts in the yard.
She carries visions of waning loved ones,
pushing walkers,
squinting at their books,
searching for thoughts that wandered off.

II
It sneaks in one night,
three inches of snow creating translucent wafers
balancing on the thinnest of branches,
white arms drooping from conifers.
Treetops silvered with filaments of ice.
Under the noon sun
slush on the driveway slides away
like turtles from their logs,
clumps of snow fall from trees—
overripe fruits decaying in flight—
ice shatters,
tiny bells ringing
ringing
the beautiful uncertainty.

III
Limbs restless, clothes heavy,
I am impatient with the deceptions:
the cold sunlight,
warm winds dragging winter on their backs.
And that moon,
hanging around well past dawn.

IV

With gait graceful as daybreak,
a fox emerges from the wood,
fur afire in the blue hour—
disappears into a thicket.
She heeds the call to tend to her young
in this season of dying and new life,
when the harsh tongue of the moon
rolls out her truth-telling light.

Liminal Space

Deep breaths of farmland sigh
across the county where she lives,
constricted by grids of asphalt,
interrupted by gasps
of new houses, strip malls, industrial parks,
front loaders and dump trucks rasping
across black soil.

Weedy patches encircle expiring barns,
caved-in roofs draped like discarded bathrobes,
skeletons partly exposed.
Vines bulge like veins from the siding,
paint curls away from its century of bonding,
whispering red.
Remnants of another life—
    reminders of the sweet scent of hay,
    the embrace of cool darkness on a hot day,
    hoof, paw, boot prints stamped in the doorway
they wait for winds to scatter their walls
like a deck of cards flung across the fields,
their groans heard only by birds.

Breathless,
with hands sheathed in tissue-thin skin,
exhaustion heavier than granite,
she teeters on her cane,
crosses a room of memories—
    the odor of firewood at the first snow,
    a colorized photo, a gift from her first beau,
    the watch she wore seventy-five years ago
her gaze lingers
at the intersection of road and horizon,
hungering for care
or permission to fall.

Lunar Eclipse

January19, 2019

8:30
The moon shines pure,
--no ordinary moon, but perigee,
so close to earth it exhales past its boundaries—
glistens the snow,
cuts shadows in crisp lines,
brings clarity to a winter night.

9:46
The moon, smudged at its bottom edge,
--no ordinary smudge, like a passing cloud,
but a stain, creeping over the white face—
lays a dirty cast on the snow,
smearing shadows—
gloom hovers.

10:16
The moon, a feeble frown of light
--nearly overcome with thickening shades,
red stain soaking through the grey—
turns snow into a dark shroud,
shadows into black holes—
the night broods in silence.

10:32
The moon gasps,
--aspirates a last flare of light—
darkens snow to eerie black—
the earth shoulders a heavy burden,
sinks into itself,
threads to its sun severed.

The Mariana Trench

The day you were buried it was ten degrees,
the ground cover a shroud of snow.

The minister was late, searching
for soil soft enough to toss into your grave.

She arrived with clay red and icy,
offered it to the mourners.

My hand, ungloved and raw, picked out a chunk,
threw it into the hole.

It landed on your coffin
with a thud.

From my pocket I drew out
a bag of ground coffee—

for we never took a trip without a thermos of coffee—
and for a time I joined you,

seven miles down into the sea,
into the deepest hole on earth,

where I drifted in darkness and silence,
wounds burning in salty waters

II

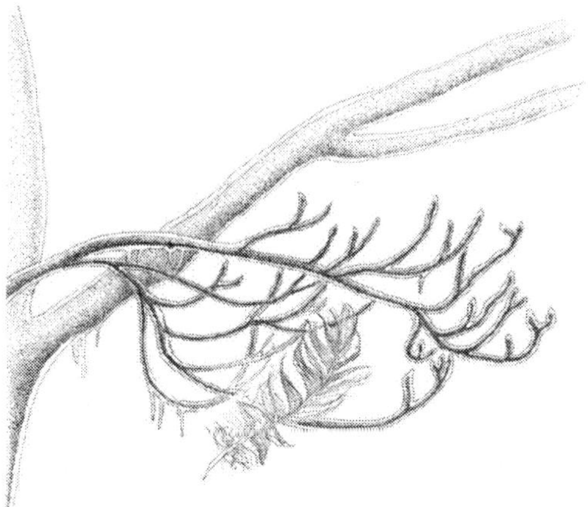

Ice Storm

It arrived in silence.
Only raindrops tapped on the roof
while night's exhale turned frigid,
fingers of ice tightening around winter-naked trees,
thickening in layers on young twigs, hopeful buds,
burden upon burden on branches.
We didn't hear the cracking of limbs,
the thud of trees felled,
the ripping, battering, beating.

Triumphant,
with the blinding brilliance of crystal,
morning sun uncloaked
branches encased in ice,
bowing in deference;
trees with gashes and wounds,
trunks twisted into grotesque shapes,
horrified expressions;
giants ripped from their soil,
lying helpless in the street,
root balls exposed.

We heard the clanging of victory:
ice cracking,
infusing the air with metallic cacophony,
releasing its grip to ride on whipping winds,
shards like flying daggers,
pelting windows,
stabbing the earth,
shattering on sidewalks—
glass underfoot.

Few dared leave their houses,
in awe of raindrops.

Lion Sister

She rests near the Serengeti road,
        indifferent to the presence of our jeep
dry grass curls around her haunches,
scars mar her face;
her ear—torn.

Preoccupied—
        lost after the little gazelle led her to parts unknown
                then disappeared
she rises—
muscles swell on her bones—
sniffs for the scent map that will take her to her pride,
circles,
sniffs again.

She climbs a tree to its sturdiest limb,
dark power silhouetted against the morning sun,
scans the deserted plain.
With precision
she positions front paws on the trunk,
leaps to the ground
landing light as a silk scarf.

Into the sun she roams
        head low
                plaintive rumbles in her throat.

Ghazal of the Lost Necklace

I found the chamber of the jewelry box empty, the necklace
lost.
She left behind so little; now her amethyst, lost.

The gem once laid on her collarbone like a child's head
resting on her mother's breast.
The child grew and pushed away, not knowing what would
be lost.

With time the amethyst faded, but not her words, "Life goes
on for the living."
Her voice getting louder with the years, after so many losses.

The year she died, roses bloomed in winter.
On my birthday, frost-tipped petals opened to loss.

A hummingbird hides in the purple fuchsia, bursts skyward at
my approach.
Memories of her erupt without warning, and I startle, for I
thought they were lost.

Her eyes blue with love, she said, "Jane, this pendant is my
gift to you."
I long for the touch of the amethyst, the tender embrace of
the chain I lost.

When autumn first opens its hand

a parade spills from its palm:
sumac berries flare, the color of wine,
goldenrod pierces a sky clear as an infant's eyes;
milkweed's silky filaments drift in the breeze,
while overhead, cranes ride the wind, trumpeting.

Scattered in the procession are the ragged and the torn:
dried stalks clack together in the gusts,
winds cast twigs in the path,
carry chills and a trace of rot.

A leaden canopy looms in the north.

The spectacle casts a spell—
I cloak myself in enchantment,
though my pockets bulge
with rusty bits of grief.

Why I go to the ocean when life veers into disorder

Approach the edge of the continent
face the wildest of the wilds:
are you not startled?
Behold the sea:
its endless hand, pressing against the horizon,
its rude shoulder, shoving at the earth,
its whispers and roars emerging
darkly from below.

And what of its accomplice, the wind?
With potent arms
it whips up deliriums,
explodes water skyward,
hurls it ashore,
then claws at the palms
tearing and shredding.

The mayhem keens day and night,
the sea and the wind,
violent revelers that will not rest.
Though bedlam swirls,
I hold my stance,
anchor my feet in the sand,
release taut lines,
discover calm waters.

The Text on Malicious Magic

looms at the back of the museum display,
a thick tome of Sumatran alchemy,
bark pages and mottled cover
tightly bound in plaited rattan,
filled with the secrets of extracting
the spirit of a captured enemy.
Penned by a datu,
who would sling his heavy volume over his shoulder,
walk from village to village,
straps cutting into his skin,
carrying the hope of healing,
and freedom.

I imagine untying its bindings,
deciphering its codes,
stealing the power of my enemies:
incantations for an aching hip,
teas for restoring dimming eyes,
potions for the return of lost words,
dances for dispersing an ever-growing parade of losses.

But the datu's magic offers no escape from suffering;
the exhibit label states a subtler purpose:
to subdue an enemy solely to acquire
its supernatural power.

A terrified Monet, losing his sight,
paints the blurred landscapes he sees:
hard edges of a bridge softened by fog
flowers blended in a recipe of explosive color
the shapes of halos

Waiting for magic,
I ease onto a bench,
close my eyes;
gather my enemies about me like a shawl.

The Feather Variations

Doloroso
A jumble on the curb:
broken table artificial Christmas tree photo albums
with one last glance at the forlorn and fractured
I drive away, heart aflutter,
basket of feathers on the passenger seat.

I.Dolce
A collection of quills abandoned in the yard,
fringed and tailored
neon blue and buff
striped, yellow-shafted,
once bathed and preened
for warmth, courtship, brooding,
for thousand-mile journeys.

II. Capriccio
I dream of books.
Five generations of hand-me-downs,
Little Women's gold spine chipped,
red bindings of *A Visit from Santa Claus*
shredded.
In a threadbare bookshop
the proprietor gathers them all, a flurry
of old stories swirling aloft…
feathers, grazing the cheeks.

III. Cantabile

The forest across the street where the calls of wood thrush
once echoed,
where flora crowded the path and darkness turned thoughts
inward,
now felled
unveiling golden grasses crowned with sunflowers,
a skyline soft and sinuous,
meadowlark song taking wing on the breeze.

IV. Jubiloso

Scent of burning leaves hovers on the wind:
birds flock,
lift off,
leave behind worn feathers,
eye the long view.

III

Lament of the Dandelion Seed

How did I get here,
drifting
over seas of deep green
past islands blaring with color
bumping against hard corners
pushed by unseen forces
in directions I never intended?

There was a time
when darkness melted away
and the soil warmed—
I was a little sun,
part of a large chorus
of bright bits of light—
Oh how loud we sang!

Now I am hardly substantial,
an insignificant filament,
ghostly pale,
silent,
tresses all atangle,
and I can only fly,
alone
trembling
                    free

Art in the Time of COVID-19

A simple arrangement—
cup, teapot, bamboo in a planter—
I pick up my pencil,
hover over the paper,
abiding emptiness.

For those sheltered at home,
a pandemic grows fat with time,
so each day I render a small bit,
darken an outline,
shade in contours.

After a week,
the cup takes shape,
leaves reach upward,
light shines among the shadows—
I learn to sketch
a still life.

Tropical Wonderland

Vegetation crowds the road like a river impatient at its banks,
flowers tower overhead,
we are four friends jouncing on a bus
plunging into tunnels of green.
Disembarking, tiny popsicles placed in our hands
before a host hurries us through a warren of buildings
across bridges, down and up stairs…
digital keys tied to our wrists open doors
to rooms of marble and mahogany.
From the balconies we glimpse a jungle,
breezes mutter in the palms,
birds call…

we are lured on,
pass bars presided over by Mad Hatters
waving bottles labeled DRINK ME—
it is always tea time here—
buffets of abundance offering
guacamole crunchy with grasshoppers,
cakes that beg EAT ME.

Cameras perch in the thicket like Cheshire cats.

We are often lost,
losing track of our Latitude and Longitude
wandering past waterfalls, pools,
into dark passageways.
"Which way? Which way?" we ask.
Our questions meet with quizzical stares,
gestures pointing in opposite directions,
an offer of horchata
before backs are turned.

Curiouser and curiouser,
we happen upon
a pandemonium of scarlet parrots
squawking imperial decrees,
a flamboyance of flamingos
honking like geese,
their beaks sturdy as croquet mallets.
We quadrille with a dolphin,
walk on the sea bottom among schools of fish
flipping around our heads like playing cards.

We awaken with a slap of winter at our home airport—
at last, a Latitude and Longitude we know—
dragging suitcases packed with memories,
or perhaps just dreams.

At Starved Rock

When frost clings to the windshield
drive misted roads
to the river swelled over its banks
where dark hulks of eagles keep watch…
step into cathedral canyons,
hike aisles of mud and half-frozen footprints
through congregations of bare oaks,
hemlocks and ferns stubbornly verdant,
limestone walls ascending,
glistening with St. Peter's sandstone—
listen to the ring of meltwater,
winds, humming—
follow the flight of the chickadee,
slide your feet with caution on frozen streams—
your limbs will remember their strength—
inhale the cleansing cold.

Round the bend.

Draped on scaffolds of rock
an altar of ice soars
milky white, aqua, blue,
creator of chasms
suspended…
choir of waters
mute.

Sing along.

Serengeti Pilgrimage

Twenty-one elephants process
single file across the endless plain,
mothers, offspring,
and their priestess—
tallest in stature,
long tusks brushing dry grasses.

Twenty-one elephants approach
the stream with ceremonial dignity,
wrinkled skin the ancient vestments of their kind.
Two teens turn to spar, short tusks locking—
an elder's trunk nudges them on.

Twenty-one elephants crowd
at the bank,
a family at table,
heads nod, ears flap,
trunks sway.

For this timeless ritual,
twenty-one elephants unroll their trunks,
glide them to the river,
the young stretch, kneel to reach the surface—
all in reverent silence
but for the splash--
the water of life.

Summer Sonatina

Early morning heat idles,
angel trumpet blooms hang
pink and frilled,
heavy on their stems;
fragrance sweet and unknown
hums in the air.
In the woods chipmunks cluck
a rhythm of incessant kisses,
declaring their devotion to these trees,
this day.

Accompanying the ostinato of afternoon heat
a storm enters reluctantly—
dragging her feet,
wind mothering her forward.
Drumming and pounding finally arrive,
gusts slap young shoots from their limbs,
push rain sideways.

Tantrum complete,
soothing rains settle in
like a woman in an easy chair,
pianissimo.

Night simmers with song;
cicada maracas rise and fall,
cricket bells pulse,
katydids brush tiny cymbals:
CH-ch-ch…
CH-ch-ch.
After the band quits for the night,
two owls hoot single note melodies
in overlapping counterpoint,
meeting in the darkness.

On the deck one August morning

a damp heat sits down like a giant bear,
slow and heavy,
a dome of warmth and drought;
wide hands of oak leaves
cast deep shadows—
when a breeze swings past,
they rouse from their meditations,
pat each other, and the wind.

A silver spotted skipper clings
to my water glass,
its dark butterfly wings closed,
climbs to the rim,
dares me to take a picture.
Before I click the shutter
it flies off,
wings laughing.

In the woods
a swoosh of feathers,
a blink of color,
and birdsong:
warbles and coos,
squawks, drumbeats.
I whistle into the layers of green,
get an answer.

In the ensuing exchange
the replies come closer,
and I stop counting time;
a duet is woven,
some wordless thread is tied—
or perhaps just recognized.
Later, I fill the birdbath,
watch robins bathe
and drink.

The Dance Unending

...and alle manner of thing shalle be welle.
Julian of Norwich (1342-c.1416)

Just before dawn
a coyote dances through the yard—
a passing zephyr blowing
toward the woods,
steps light as a cottonwood seed—
when the dark hulk of a turkey
rises up
spreads its winged cape,
and with two flaps,
its dance equal in grace to its pursuer,
lifts into the crook of a tree,
master of the wind.

On Turning 71

Like a boy awaiting dismissal from the dinner table,
October winds wiggle and fidget,
jiggle leaves into rogue flights,
restless breaths clearing summer's haze
revealing trees haloed in gold and fire,
shrubs flamboyant in orange.

Darkness a vise crowding both sides of the day.

Embracing the waning light
two girls run down the street,
blond waves streaming,
shouts urgent.
Halloween approaches,
they promise to show up at my door—
one a feather of a girl,
grown bulky in football uniform;
the other, sweet as a fawn in the grass,
transformed into a killer bride.

Breezes keen in the trees,
oracles warning
of snowfields vast and impassive
waiting at their edges—
no hint of what lies beneath
or beyond.

But today, nothing to do but
inhale the sweetness of apples past their prime,
yield to the insistence of the wind.

Cloud Forest

The dirt path slithers up the mountain,
teasing edges:
landslides on one side,
descents steepening on the other.
Jungle throngs the margin like parade watchers,
a pressing exuberance of foliage,
spiky bromeliads perched on tree limbs,
banana leaves waving like flags.
I climb, catch glimpses
of the mountains,
mists wafting like shades,
snagged on peaks;
ragged skirts concealing crags and cliffs,
seeming to alter the topography;
then shape-shifting
into streams of gauze flowing downward,
turning valleys into smoky cauldrons,
unveiling the rugged slopes,
their verdant hues and relentless abundance.

I didn't see it coming.
Rounding a corner
I am embraced by a cloud,
enrobed in downy grey,
moist fingers on my cheeks,
vision shrouded.
The mountain and I swept
into the bosom of a wraith,
immersed in sweet drizzle.
Destination abandoned,
I stand becalmed,
thoughts adrift
like floating droplets,
consider…

the breath of mists:
the thickening and thinning,
grasping and releasing,
soaring then plummeting,
gathering only to dissolve,
a life measured
in the rhythms of a cloud.

Acknowledgments

I extend my sincere gratitude to the editors of the following print and online journals for the previous publications of these poems, in their same or slightly altered forms:

after hours: a journal of Chicago writing and art: "Ghazal of the Lost Necklace", "When autumn first opens its hand", "Wolf Moon", "Liminal Space"
Glacial Hills Review: "The Mariana Trench"
Gyroscope: "On Turning 71"
Plum Tree Tavern: "Lunar Eclipse"
Red Eft Review: "North Country Trail", "Serengeti Pilgrimage"
The Rockford Review: "On the deck one August morning", "Ice Storm", "Tropical Wonderland"
Snowy Egret: "Lion Sister"
The Weekly Avocet: "The Bluebird Trail", "Why I go to the ocean when life veers into disorder"
Willow Review: "Art in the Time of COVID-19"

I wish to thank my instructors and poetry companions at Second Saturday Poetry Workshop, The Clearing, and Tree of Life poetry group. Their guidance resonates in these poems. I am deeply grateful to my partner, Neil Whitman, who is always willing to attend a poetry event, unravel a computer knot, and listen.

Made in the USA
Monee, IL
19 April 2024

56857456R00026